THEORY IS FUN

BOOK I

by

DAVID HIRSCHBERG

Illustrations and Cartoons by

FRANK LITTLE

EL2501

Dedicated

to all

My Young Music Friends

THE STAFF

5th LINE	
4th LINE	4th SPACE
3rd LINE	3rd SPACE
2nd LINE	2nd SPACE
1st LINE	1st SPACE

There are 5 lines in a Staff.
There are also 4 spaces in a Staff.
Both the lines and spaces are counted from the bottom to the top.

FILL IN THE FOLLOWING:
There are .... lines in a Staff.
There are .... spaces in a Staff.
Both the lines and spaces are counted from the bottom to the ....
Exercise: Draw your own staff.

EXERCISES ON LINES

Put a small circle around each line like this:

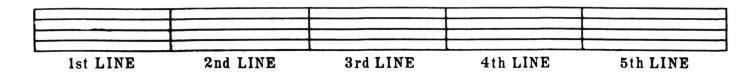

| 1st LINE | 2nd LINE | 3rd LINE | 4th LINE | 5th LINE |

EXERCISES IN SPACES

Put a small circle in each space like this: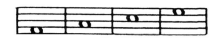

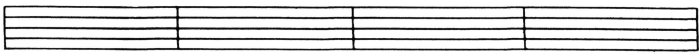

| 1st SPACE | 2nd SPACE | 3rd SPACE | 4th SPACE |

LINES AND SPACES

In the following exercises the circles appearing on the lines and in the spaces are referred to as WHOLE NOTES.

Exercise: Write in the number of the line directly under each note. For example: the number 2 under the first note means that the note is on the second line.
The number 5 under the next note means that the note is on the fifth line. Go through this entire exercise putting in the numbers under the notes.

Exercise: Write in the number of the space directly under each note. For example: the number 1 under the first note means that the note is in the first space.
The number 4 under the next note means that the note is in the fourth space. Go through this entire exercise putting in the numbers under the notes.

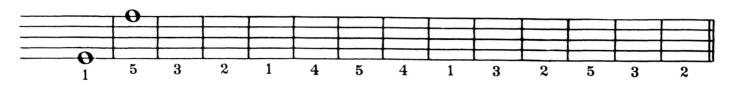

Exercise: Write a note on the line indicated by the number. Thus a number 1 means that you are to write a note on the first line.

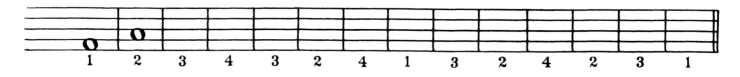

Exercise: Write a note in the space indicated by the number. Thus a number 2 means that you are to write a note in the second space.

THE TREBLE CLEF SIGN

HOW TO DRAW IT

FIRST STEP

Exercise: Copy this a few times.

SECOND STEP

Exercise: Copy this a few times.

THIRD STEP

Exercise: Copy this a few times.

FOURTH STEP

Exercise: Copy this a few times.

FIFTH STEP

Exercise: Copy this a few times.

MUSICAL PICTURE PUZZLES

Find the Treble Clef sign in each picture

TREBLE CLEF NOTES ON LINES

NAMES OF LINES. Each line in the Treble Clef has its own name. The first line is called E, the second line is called G, the third line is called B, the fourth line is called D and the fifth line is called F.

Exercise: Make up a five word sentence in which the first word begins with E, the second word begins with G, the third word begins with B, the fourth word begins with D and the fifth word begins with F. Example: Every Good Boy Deserves Fun.

Write your own sentence here:
E .... G .... B .... D .... F ....

Exercise: Write the names below the following notes:

MUSICAL SPELLING PUZZLES

ON TREBLE CLEF LINES

WHAT TO DO!

Look at each picture below and then write in the Treble Clef line notes which tell what the picture is. For example: the first picture is an egg so we write the three notes E-G-G. Do the same with all the pictures.

EXAMPLE:

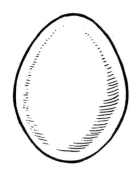

This is an
E G G
so we write
the following notes:

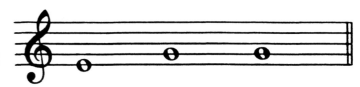

Do the same with the following:

This is a
_ _ _
so we write
the following notes:

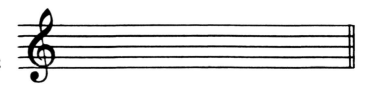

This is a
_ _ _
so we write
the following notes:

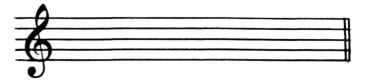

EL2501

TREBLE CLEF NOTES IN SPACES

NAMES OF SPACES. Each space in the Treble Clef has its own name. The first space is called F, the second space is called A, the third space is called C and the fourth space is called E.

Question: The above four letters spell a word. What is that word?

Exercise: Write the word four times:

....

Exercise: Write the names below the following notes:

MUSICAL SPELLING PUZZLES
IN TREBLE CLEF SPACES

WHAT TO DO!

Look at each picture below and then write in the Treble Clef space notes which tell what the picture is. For example: the first picture is a playing card known as an ACE so we write the three notes A-C-E. Do the same with all the pictures.

EXAMPLE:

This is an
A C E
so we write
the following notes:

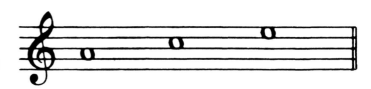

Do the same with the following:

This is a

_ _ _ _
so we write
the following notes:

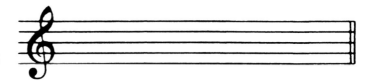

This is a

_ _ _ _
so we write
the following notes:

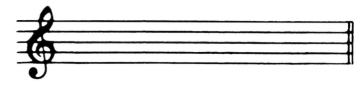

A STORY IN MUSIC-TREBLE CLEF

In the following story certain words are spelled out in musical notation. First find out what word each group of notes stands for. Then go back and read the story. Write the missing words down below.

MY GOOD DEED

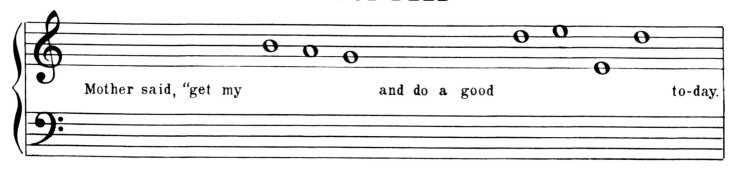

Mother said, "get my _____ and do a good _____ to-day.

Go and buy an _____ an some _____ for me.

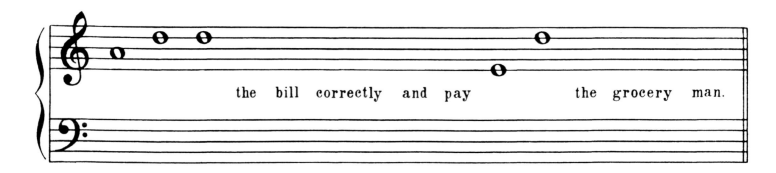

the bill correctly and pay _____ the grocery man.

The words written in music language were ____, ____, ____, ____, ____, ____, ____, ____, ____, ____, ____, ____, ____,

THE BASS CLEF SIGN
HOW TO DRAW IT

FIRST STEP

Exercise: Copy this a few times.

SECOND STEP

Exercise: Copy this a few times.

THIRD STEP

Exercise: Copy this a few times.

FOURTH STEP

Exercise: Copy this a few times.

MUSICAL PICTURE PUZZLES
Find the Bass Clef sign in each picture

BASS CLEF NOTES ON LINES

NAMES OF LINES. Each line in the Bass Clef has its own name. The first line is called G, the second line is B, the third line is called D, the fourth line is called F and the fifth line is called A.

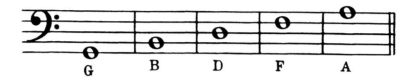

Exercise: Make up a five word sentence in which the first word begins with G, the second word begins with B, the third word begins with D, the fourth word begins with F and the fifth word begins with A. Example: Growling Bears Don't Fear Anyone.

Write your own sentence here.
G_____ B_____ D_____ F_____ A_____

Exercise: Write the names below the following notes:

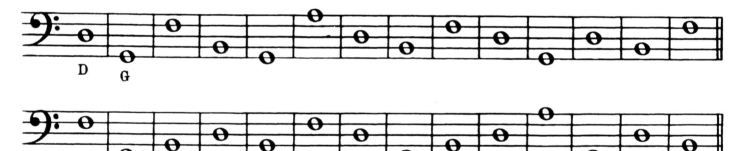

BASS CLEF NOTES IN SPACES

NAMES OF SPACES. Each space in the Bass Clef has its own name. The first space is called A, the second space is called C, the third space is called E and the fourth space is called G.

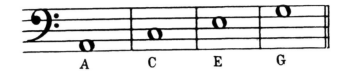

Exercise: Make up a four word sentence in which the first word begins with A, the second word begins with C, the third word begins with E and the fourth word begins with G. Example: All Cows Eat Grass.

Write your own sentence here.
A................ C................ E................ G................

Exercise: Write the names below the following notes:

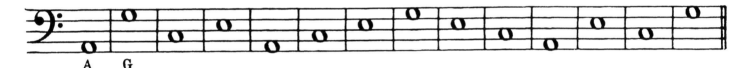

MUSICAL SPELLING PUZZLES
IN THE BASS CLEF

WHAT TO DO !

Look at each picture below and then write in the Bass Clef lines or spaces which tell what the picture is. For example: the first picture is a policeman's BADGE. So we write the five notes B-A-D-G-E. Do the same with all the pictures.

EXAMPLE:

This is a
B A D G E
so we write the
following notes :

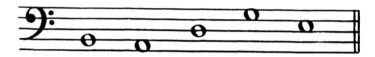

Do the same with the following:

This is a
_ _ _ _
so we write the
following notes :

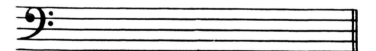

This is a
_ _ _ _ _ _
so we write the
following notes :

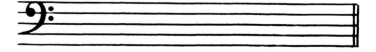

A STORY IN MUSIC - BASS CLEF

In the following story certain words are spelled out with groups of notes. Each group of notes stands for a word. First find out what these words are. Then go back and read the story. Write the missing words below.

IN A ZOO

In a zoo I saw them _____ the lions in _____ big

One was very _____ He _____ me and roared.

I am not _____ ," I said. Then I _____ away.

The words written in music language are:

....

TREBLE CLEF AND BASS CLEF
THE GRAND STAFF

Whenever two staffs of music are presented together at the same time they are joined together with a brace and the entire combination is known as a Grand Staff. Study the Grand Staff below so that you will be able to do the exercises which follow.

Exercise: Complete this Grand Staff 3 times in the following places.

Exercise: Write the names of the following notes.

Exercise: Write the following notes.

B   C   D   G   A   E   F   A   B   E   G   F   C

A STORY IN MUSIC

BASS AND TREBLE CLEF

THE BEE IN MY GARDEN

One day I saw a   He was in   flower

I called my   He is not   my

said. I   him to chase the

before it stung my   and   on me.

The words written in music language are: ....

....

HOW TO WRITE NOTES
WHOLE-HALF-QUARTER-EIGHTH

WHOLE NOTES

1) Draw a circle.

Exercise: Write a few whole notes.

HALF NOTES

1) Draw a circle.
2) Add a stem.

Exercise: Write a few half notes.

QUARTER NOTES

1) Draw a circle.
2) Add a stem.
3) Fill in the circle.

Exercise: Write a few quarter notes.

EIGHTH NOTES

1) Draw two circles.
2) Add the stems.
3) Fill in the circles.
4) Join the stems.

Exercise: Write a few eighth notes in groups of two.

EIGHTH NOTE

(*Single note*)

As above, only add a hook to each stem.

Exercise: Write a few single eighth notes.

STEMS UP!–STEMS DOWN!

WHEN STEMS GO UP!

All notes below the third line have stems going up on the right side.

WHEN STEMS GO DOWN!

All notes on or above the third line have stems going down on the left side.

REMEMBER: In doing the following exercises remember the above rules.

Exercise: Change to half notes. *See page 18*

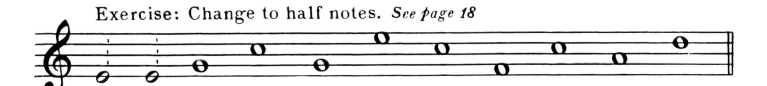

Exercise: Change to quarter notes. *See page 18*

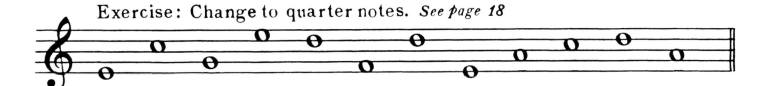

Exercise: Change to eighth notes in groups of two. *See page 18*

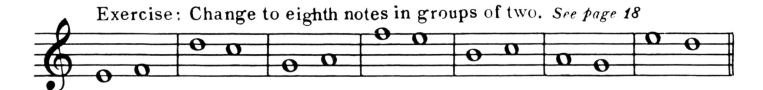

Exercise: Change to single eighth notes. *See page 18*

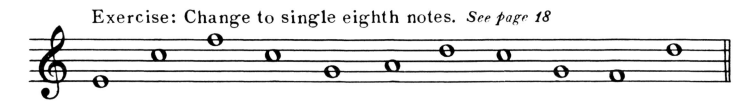

TIME VALUES OF NOTES
IN $\frac{4}{4}$ - $\frac{3}{4}$ - $\frac{2}{4}$ TIME

○ WHOLE NOTE..4 COUNTS

𝅗𝅥· DOTTED HALF NOTE....................................3 COUNTS

𝅗𝅥 HALF NOTE...2 COUNTS

♩· DOTTED QUARTER NOTE.....................1½ COUNTS

♩ QUARTER NOTE...1 COUNT

♫ EIGHTH NOTES.................... Two eighth notes equal to....1 COUNT

♪ EIGHTH NOTE (Single one)..........................½ COUNT

Exercise: Write underneath each note how many counts it receives.

4 COUNTS   2 COUNTS

RHYTHM   TIME SIGNATURES

Music, as we know it today. consists of three important factors --- RHYTHM, MELODY and HARMONY. In the history of music we know that first came RHYTHM. The savages with their drums and dances made use of RHYTHM even before MELODY was added. It is only at a much later date in the history of music that HARMONY came into being. It is, therefore. essential that the RHYTHM in each piece of music be first felt before further study.

March around the room in March Time and count 1 - 2 - 3 - 4, 1 - 2 - 3 - 4, etc. Each such group is called a measure. Be sure to stress the first count in every measure. We call this FOUR QUARTER TIME. For a further explanation of this look at the lower part of the page.

Dance around the room in Waltz Time and count 1 - 2 - 3, 1 - 2 - 3, etc. while you are dancing. Be sure to stress the first count in every measure. We call this THREE QUARTER TIME. For a further explanation of this look at the lower part of the page.

FOUR QUARTER TIME
Four counts to a measure
One count for every quarter note.
Count 1 - 2 - 3 - 4 in every measure.

THREE QUARTER TIME
Three counts to a measure.
One count for every quarter note.
Count 1 - 2 - 3 in every measure.

TWO QUARTER TIME.
Two counts to a measure.
One count for every quarter note.
Count 1 - 2 in every measure.

HOW TO COUNT
WHOLE NOTES, DOTTED HALF NOTES, HALF NOTES

 When we see a whole note we count 1-2-3-4

Exercise: Write in the counting below each note.

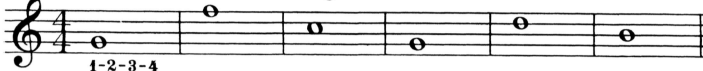

 When we see a dotted half note we count 1-2-3

Exercise: Write in the counting.

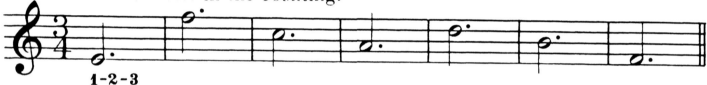

 When we see a half note we count 1-2

Exercise: Write in the counting.

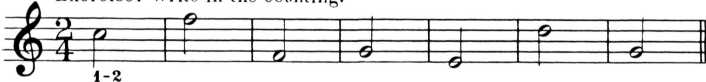

HOW TO COUNT
SIMPLE COMBINATIONS IN ⁴/₄ TIME

In FOUR QUARTER TIME there are some simple time value combinations which are very important.

WHOLE NOTES ONLY.

One whole note to a measure.

Count 1 - 2 - 3 - 4 for each whole note.

Count 1 - 2 - 3 - 4 in every measure.

HALF NOTES ONLY.

Two half notes to a measure.

Count 1 - 2 on the first half note.

Count 3 - 4 on the next half note.

Count 1 - 2 - 3 - 4 in every measure.

Exercise: Write in the counting below each note.

QUARTER NOTES ONLY.

Four quarter notes to a measure.

One count on each note.

Count 1 - 2 - 3 - 4 in every measure.

Exercise: Write in the counting below each note.

EIGHTH NOTES ONLY.

Eight eighth notes to a measure.

One count for each group of two eighth notes.

Count 1 - 2 - 3 - 4 in every measure.

Exercise: Write in the counting below each note.

HOW TO COUNT
SIMPLE COMBINATIONS IN ¾ TIME

In THREE QUARTER TIME there are some simple time value combinations which are very important.

DOTTED HALF NOTES ONLY.
One dotted half note to a measure.
Count 1 - 2 - 3 - for each dotted half note.
Count 1 - 2 - 3 in every measure.

Exercise: Write in the counting below each note.

QUARTER NOTES ONLY.
Three quarter notes to a measure.
One count on each note.
Count 1 - 2 - 3 in every measure.

Exercise: Write in the counting below each note.

EIGHTH NOTES ONLY.
Six eighth notes to a measure.
One count for each group of two eighth notes.
Count 1 - 2 - 3 in every measure.

Exercise: Write in the counting below each note.

HOW TO COUNT
SIMPLE COMBINATIONS IN ²⁄₄ TIME

In TWO QUARTER TIME there are some simple time value combinations which are very important.

HALF NOTES ONLY.
One half note to a measure.
Count 1 - 2 for each half note.
Count 1 - 2 in every measure.

Exercise: Write in the counting below each note.

QUARTER NOTES ONLY.
Two quarter notes to a measure.
One count on each note.
Count 1 - 2 in every measure.

Exercise: Write in the counting below each note.

EIGHTH NOTES ONLY
Four eighth notes to a measure.
One count for each group of two eighth notes.
Count 1 - 2 in every measure.

Exercise: Write in the counting below each note.

MEASURES - BAR LINES

In FOUR QUARTER TIME there are four beats to every measure. After each group of four beats we draw a bar line. When we come to the end of any piece of music, we draw a double bar line.
Example:

Exercise: Complete the following measures by putting in bar lines in the proper places.

In THREE QUARTER TIME there are three beats to every measure. After each group of three beats we draw a bar line.
Exercise: Complete the following measures by putting in bar lines in the proper places.

In TWO QUARTER TIME there are two beats to every measure. After each group of two beats we draw a bar line.
Exercise: Complete the following measures by putting in bar lines in the proper places.

Exercise: Complete the following measures by putting in bar lines in the proper places.

Exercise: Here are some famous bits of melodies. Put in the proper time signatures. Can you name these melodies?

HOW TO WRITE RESTS
WHOLE - HALF - QUARTER - EIGHTHS

WHOLE RESTS

Draw a black
box hanging down
from the 4th line.

Exercise: Write a few whole rests

HALF RESTS

Draw a black
box sitting on
the 3rd line.

Exercise: Write a few half rests

QUARTER RESTS

This looks like
a bird with
wings spread.

Exercise: Write a few quarter rests

EIGHTH RESTS

This looks like a
little flag. It also
looks like a number 7.

Exercise: Write a few eighth rests

Exercise: Write underneath each rest the kind of a rest it is.

REST EQUIVALENTS
OF WHOLE NOTES-HALF NOTES
QUARTER NOTES-EIGHTH NOTES

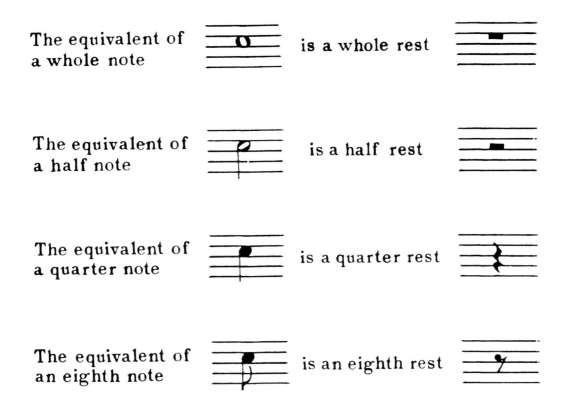

The equivalent of a whole note — is a whole rest

The equivalent of a half note — is a half rest

The equivalent of a quarter note — is a quarter rest

The equivalent of an eighth note — is an eighth rest

Exercise: Write underneath each note it's equivalent value as a rest.

Exercise: Write above each rest it's equivalent value as a note.

TIME VALUE OF RESTS

IN 4/4 3/4 2/4 TIME

WHOLE REST ....
- in 4/4 = 4 COUNTS
- in 3/4 = 3 COUNTS
- in 2/4 = 2 COUNTS

HALF REST .... 2 COUNTS

QUARTER REST .... 1 COUNT

EIGHTH REST .... 1/2 COUNT

Exercise: Write underneath each rest how many counts it receives.

2 Counts 1 Count 1/2 Count

HOW TO COUNT WHOLE RESTS

In FOUR QUARTER TIME we count 1 - 2 - 3 - 4 - for a whole rest.
Exercise: Write in the counting.

In THREE QUARTER TIME we count 1 - 2 - 3 for a whole rest.
Exercise: Write in the counting.

In TWO QUARTER TIME we count 1 - 2 for a whole rest.

Exercise: Write in the counting.

HOW TO COUNT HALF RESTS

A HALF REST most frequently appears in four quarter time. It always get two counts in this time signature.

1-2-3-4

Exercise: Write in the counting.

1-2-3-4

HOW TO COUNT QUARTER RESTS

A QUARTER REST appears frequently in four quarter, three quarter, and two quarter time. It gets one count in these time signatures.

1-2-3-4

Exercise: Write in the counting. Can you name these melodies?

COMPLETING MEASURES
PUTTING IN BAR LINES - RESTS - TIME SIGNATURES

Exercise: Put in the Bar Lines.

Exercise: Put in the proper Rests where the x appears.

Exercise: Put in the counting and the TIME SIGNATURES

SHARPS IN SPACES

Here is a SHARP written in a space. Notice that the little box in the middle of the SHARP is in the space. Since this space is called C, we therefore call the SHARP – C sharp.

Exercise: Write in the names of the following sharps:

E♯   A♯

Exercise: Write in the correct sharps which correspond to the given letter names.

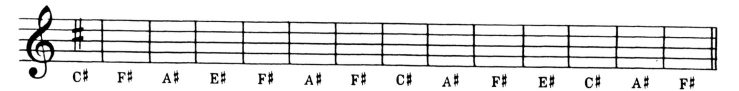

C♯   F♯   A♯   E♯   F♯   A♯   F♯   C♯   A♯   F♯   E♯   C♯   A♯   F♯

SHARPS ON LINES

Here is a SHARP written on a line. Notice that the little box in the middle of the SHARP has a staff line running through it's center. Since this line is called F, we therefore call the SHARP – F sharp.

Exercise: Write in the names of the following sharps:

F♯   G♯

Exercise: Write in the correct sharps which correspond to the given letter names.

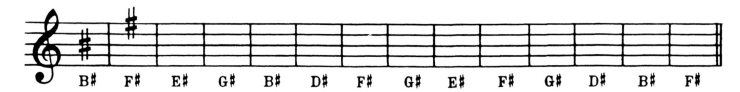

B♯   F♯   E♯   G♯   B♯   D♯   F♯   G♯   E♯   F♯   G♯   D♯   B♯   F♯

Exercise: Write in the missing notes in the Bass Clef which correspond to the ones in the Treble Clef. Write them in the Bass Clef directly underneath the Treble Clef notes in the same box. Thus if the Treble Clef has C sharp, you are to write in a C sharp note in the Bass Clef, etc. (Use whole notes).

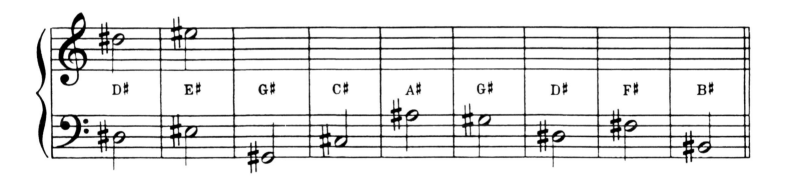

Exercise: Write in the missing notes in the Treble Clef which correspond to the ones in the Bass Clef. Write them in the Treble Clef directly above the Bass Clef notes in the same box. Thus if the Bass Clef has G sharp, you are to write in a G sharp note in the Treble Clef, etc. (Use half notes).

Exercise: Write in the missing notes in both the Treble and Bass Clefs. (Use quarter notes)

FLATS IN SPACES

Here is a FLAT written in a space. Notice that the open part of the FLAT is in the space. Since this space is called **A** we therefore call the FLAT – **A** flat.

Exercise: Write in the names of the following Flats:

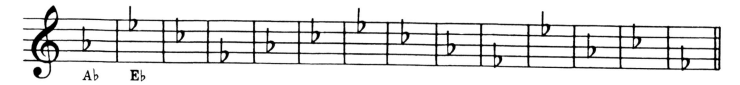

Ab Eb

Exercise: Write in the flats which correspond to the given letter names.

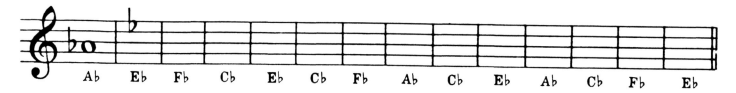

Ab Eb Fb Cb Eb Cb Fb Ab Cb Eb Ab Cb Fb Eb

FLATS ON LINES

Here is a FLAT written on a line. Notice that the open part of the FLAT has a staff line running through it's center. Since this line is called **B** we therefore call the FLAT – **B** flat.

Exercise: Write in the names of the following Flats:

Bb Db

Exercise: Write in the flats which correspond to the given letter names.

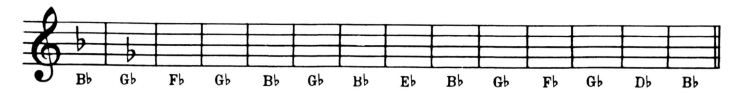

Bb Gb Fb Gb Bb Gb Bb Eb Bb Gb Fb Gb Db Bb

Exercise: Write in the missing notes in the Bass Clef which correspond to the ones in the Treble Clef. Write them in the Bass Clef directly underneath the Treble Clef notes in the same box. Thus, if the Treble Clef has G flat, you are to write a G flat in the Bass Clef, etc. (Use half notes).

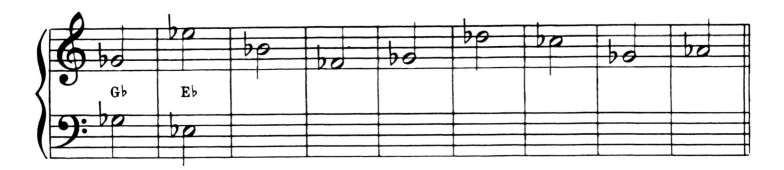

Exercise: Write in the missing notes in the Treble Clef which correspond to the ones in the Bass Clef. Write them in the Treble Clef directly above the Bass Clef notes in the same box. Thus, if the Bass Clef has D flat, you are to write a D flat in the Treble Clef, etc. (Use quarter notes).

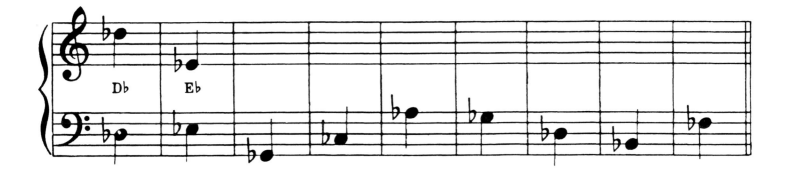

Exercise: Write in the required notes in both the Treble and Bass Clefs. (use whole notes).

NATURALS IN SPACES

Here is a NATURAL written in a space. Notice that the little box in the middle of the NATURAL is in the space. Since this space is called C, we therefore call the NATURAL – C natural.

Exercise: Write in the names of the following Naturals.

A♮   E♮

Exercise: Write in the Naturals which correspond to the given letter names.

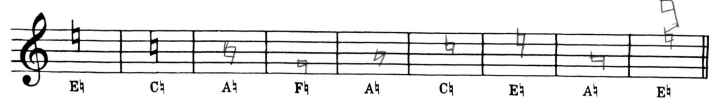

E♮   C♮   A♮   F♮   A♮   C♮   E♮   A♮   E♮

NATURALS ON LINES

Here is a NATURAL written on a line. Notice that the little box of the NATURAL has a staff line running through it. Since this line is called B, we therefore call the NATURAL – B natural.

Exercise: Write in the names of the following Naturals.

B♮   D♮

Exercise: Write in the Naturals which correspond to the given letter names.

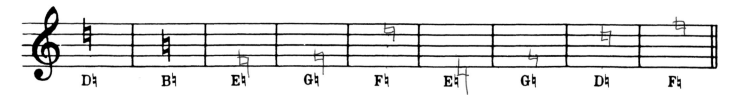

D♮   B♮   E♮   G♮   F♮   E♮   G♮   D♮   F♮

EXERCISE: Write in the missing notes in the Bass Clef which correspond to the ones in the Treble Clef. Write them in the Bass Clef directly underneath the Treble Clef notes in the same box. Thus, if the Treble Clef has G natural, you are to write a G natural in the Bass Clef, etc. (Use dotted half notes).

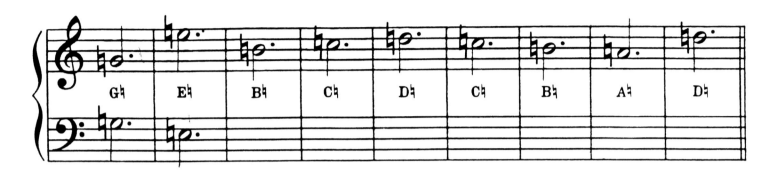

Exercise: Write in the missing notes in the Treble Clef which correspond to the ones in the Bass Clef. Write them in the Treble Clef directly above the Bass Clef notes in the same box. Thus, if the Bass Clef has D natural, you are to write a D natural in the Treble Clef, etc. (Use eighth notes).

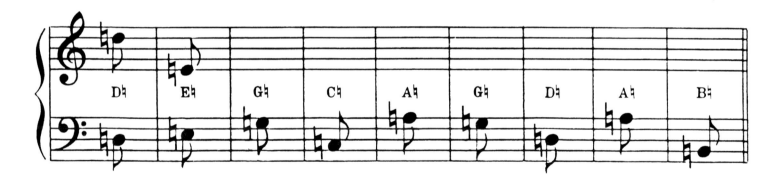

Exercise: Write in the required notes in both the Treble and Bass Clefs. (use whole notes).

LEGER LINES
BELOW THE TREBLE CLEF

Copy this note D a few times.

Copy this note C a few times.

Copy this note B a few times.

Copy this note A a few times.

Exercise: Fill in the names of the following notes:

LEGER LINES

ABOVE THE TREBLE CLEF

Copy this note G a few times.

Copy this note A a few times.

Copy this note B a few times.

Copy this note C a few times.

Exercise: Fill in the names of the following notes:

LEGER LINES
BELOW THE BASS CLEF

Exercise: Fill in the names of the following notes:

LEGER LINES
ABOVE THE BASS CLEF

HALF-STEPS

Music as it appears today in the Western World consists of the following letter-name Tones.

ASCENDING – A - A# - B - C - C# - D - D# - E - F - F# - G - G#
(B#)   (E#)

DESCENDING - G - G^b - F - E - E^b - D - D^b - C - B - B^b - A - A^b
(F^b)   (C^b)

HALF - STEPS ASCENDING USING SHARPS

When we ascend from one tone to another adjacent tone we are going a half step higher. We put a sharp on the higher tone in most instances.
Examples: A to A sharp, C to C sharp, D to D sharp, F to F sharp, G to G sharp.

HALF - STEPS ASCENDING WITHOUT USING SHARPS.

Sometimes notes are a half step apart ascending without the use of a sharp.

Example   B to C

Exercise: Answer the following questions by writing in YES or NO in the correct right hand columns.

	YES	NO
Is A to A sharp a half step apart?		
Is B to C sharp a half step apart?		
Is D to D sharp a half step apart?		
Is E to F sharp a half step apart?		
Is F to G sharp a half step apart?		
Is F to F sharp a half step apart?		

Exercise: Complete the following statements by writing in the correct answers where the dotted lines appear. Use ascending examples only. You may use sharps.

C to .... is a half step apart.   C sharp to .... is a half step apart.
D to .... is a half step apart.   D sharp to .... is a half step apart.
E to .... is a half step apart.   F sharp to .... is a half step apart.
F to .... is a half step apart.   G sharp to .... is a half step apart.
G to .... is a half step apart.   A sharp to .... is a half step apart.
A to .... is a half step apart.
B to .... is a half step apart.

HALF-STEPS DESCENDING USING FLATS

When we descend from one tone to another adjacent tone we are going a half step lower. We put a flat on the lower tone in most instances.

Examples: G to G flat, E to E flat, D to D flat, B to B flat and A to A flat.

HALF - STEPS DESCENDING WITHOUT USING FLATS

Sometimes notes are a half step apart descending without the use of a flat.

Examples: F to E and C to B.

Exercise: Answer the following questions by writing in YES or NO in the correct right hand columns.

	YES	NO
Is G to G flat a half step apart?		
Is G to F a half step apart?		
Is F to E a half step apart?		
Is D to C a half step apart?		
Is D to D flat a half step apart?		
Is C to B flat a half step apart?		
Is A to A flat a half step apart?		
Is C to B a half step apart?		

Exercise: Complete the following statements by writing in the correct answers where the dotted lines appear. Use descending examples only. Do not use sharps in your answers.

C to .... is a half step apart.

D to .... is a half step apart.

E to .... is a half step apart.

F to .... is a half step apart.

G to .... is a half step apart.

A to .... is a half step apart.

B to .... is a half step apart.

D flat to .... is a half step apart.

E flat to .... is a half step apart.

G flat to .... is a half step apart.

A flat to .... is a half step apart.

B flat to .... is a half step apart.

WHOLE-STEPS

When there is one (and only one) tone in between any of our letter-name tones then we have a WHOLE STEP.

Example: C to D is a whole step because there is one tone between them, that is, C sharp. Likewise the following are a whole step apart. D to E, F to G, G to A, A to B, E to F sharp, C to B flat, etc.

Exercise: Write in the name of the tone that you find between the following:
Between D and E there is a tone called _____
Between F and G there is a tone called _____
Between G and A there is a tone called _____
Between A and B there is a tone called _____

The following exercises are a little more difficult so be very careful.

Exercise: Write in the name of the tone that you find between the following:
Between C sharp and D sharp there is a tone called _____
Between F sharp and G sharp there is a tone called _____
Between G sharp and A sharp there is a tone called _____
Between B flat and A flat there is a tone called _____
Between E flat and D flat there is a tone called _____

Between E and F sharp there is a tone called _____
Between B and C sharp there is a tone called _____
Between F and E flat there is a tone called _____
Between C and B flat there is a tone called _____

In the following exercises you are called upon to further show your knowledge of whole steps.

Exercise: Complete the following by writing in YES or NO in the right hand columns:

	YES	NO
Is A to B a whole step?		
Is E to F a whole step?		
Is F to G a whole step?		
Is G to G sharp a whole step?		
Is C to B a whole step?		
Is C to B flat a whole step?		
Is A to G a whole step?		
Is D to D sharp a whole step?		
Is E to F sharp a whole step?		

HALF-STEPS AND WHOLE-STEPS

Exercise: Put a circle around those groups of notes which are a half step apart.

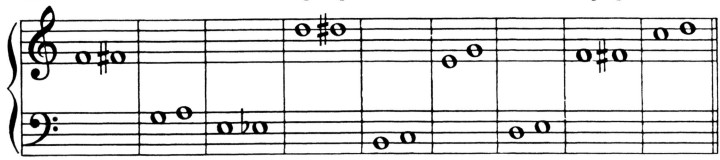

Exercise: Put a circle around those groups of notes which are a whole step apart.

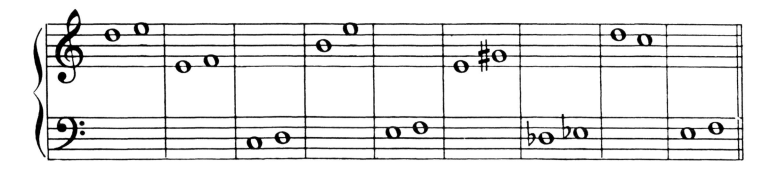